BBQ Recipes

Barbecue Cookbook For Delicious And Flavorful Barbeque

Aaron Wilson

TERMS & CONDITIONS

TABLE OF CONTENTS

Chapter 1 – BBQ Recipes Cookbook 1

Nostalgic Asian Inspired Chicken Wings...2

Best Chicken Legs Quarters 5

Vintage Grilled Skirt Steak (Churrasco)...................................9

Lucky Raspberry BBQ Sauce....12

Happy Beer Can Chicken with KC Rub...15

Great Sliced Brisket Heroes with Memphis Slaw 18

Fantastic Beer Can Chicken......21

Delightful Red Army Sauce 24

Super Red Army Sauce.............26

Awesome Barbecued asparagus with prosciutto...........................28

Iconic Summertime Dinner Hens 30

Ultimate Smoked Turkey Legs ..32

Unique Churrasco Steak Kebab with Chimichurri sauce 35

Yummy Plum BBQ Sauce 38

Tasty Buttermilk-Fried Chicken Sliders...................................41

Titanic Lazy Memphis Night Meatloaf..................................44

Rich BBQ Chicken Quarters......47

Elegant Canadian Thin Maple BBQ Sauce 50

Wonderful Canadian Thin Maple BBQ Sauce 52

Quick Teriyaki tofu kebabs 54

Awesome Favorite Whole Turkey 56

Legendary Smoked Turkey Breast 59

Excellent Lechon Liempo or Filipino Roasted Pork Belly 62

Astonishing Apricot BBQ Sauce 64

Great Lemon Pepper BBQ Grilled Chicken.................................67

Happy Smokey BBQ Chicken and Bottom Barrel Baked Beans 70

Lucky All-Purpose Chicken & Fish Marinade.................................73

Vintage Alcatraz BBQ Sauce 75

Best Alcatraz BBQ Sauce 77

Nostalgic Pepper steak with tomatoes.....................................79

Mighty Thanksgiving Turkey......81

King sized Beer Chicken 84

Crazy Filipino Skewered Banana ketchup Pork Shoulder BBQ 87

Pinnacle Mango-Habanero BBQ Sauce 89

Perfect Barbecued Wild Turkey .91

Dashing Dry Rubbed Chicken w/ Cornbread and Sausage Stuffing 94

Reliable Whole Spit-Grilled Chicken..98

Charming Smokey Coffee Sauce 101

Energetic Smokey Coffee Sauce 103

Chapter 1 – BBQ Recipes Cookbook

Thanks for purchasing this book. Now go ahead and check out these amazing barbecue recipes.

Nostalgic Asian Inspired Chicken Wings

Stupidly simple...

Ingredients:

- 2 crushed garlic cloves
- 1 tablespoon lightly toasted sesame seeds
- About 3.5 tablespoons hoisin sauce
- 1/2 teaspoon ginger powder
- 2 tablespoons soy sauce
- 1 tablespoon honey
- About 1.5 teaspoon dark sesame oil
- 2 pound chicken wings

Directions:

1. First of all, please assemble all the ingredients at one place. Preheat the pallet grill to about 210 to 220 degrees F.

2. Now arrange the wings onto the lower rack of pallet grill & cook properly for about 1.5 hours.

3. Meanwhile, in a large bowl, mix together remaining all ingredients.

4. This step is important. Remove wings from pallet grill & place in the bowl of garlic mixture.

5. Then coat wings with garlic mixture generously.

6. Now, set the pallet grill to about 360 to 370 degrees F.

7. Arrange coated wings onto a foil lined baking sheet & sprinkle with sesame seeds.

8. One thing remains to be done. Now place the pan onto the lower rack of pallet grill & cook, covered for about 25 to 30 minutes.

9. Finally serve immediately.

Be unique, be extraordinary…

Per Serving:

Calories: 508

Fat: 19.6g

Carbs: 12.4g

Protein: 67.2g

Best Chicken Legs Quarters

Something is special!!

Ingredients:

- 1/3 cup of fresh orange juice
- Salt
- 1/3 cup of olive oil
- Black pepper
- About 1/4 cup of fresh oregano leaves, finely chopped
- 1/4 cup of fresh lime juice
- 1 bunch of fresh cilantro
- About 1.5 teaspoons of cumin
- 1 tablespoon of orange zest
- About 1.5 tablespoon of lime zest
- 6 cloves of garlic
- 5 1/2 pounds of chicken legs quarters

Directions:

1. First of all, please assemble all the ingredients at one place. Season the chicken legs with some salt & pepper then set it aside.

2. Then quickly combine the rest of the ingredients in a food processor & blend them smooth to make the marinade.

3. Next, please set 1/2 cup of the marinade aside & toss the rest of it with the chicken legs in a medium or large mixing bowl.

4. This step is important. Quickly cover the chicken legs & refrigerate them for about 4 to 6 h or an overnight.

5. Now preheat the smoker on 390 to 400 F.

6. Cover each chicken leg with a piece of foil & poke several holes in each one of them.

7. Then smoke the chicken legs for 1 h 30 to 35 min to 2 h or until they register 165 F while turning every once in a while.

8. One thing remains to be done. Once the time is up, transfer the chicken legs to a heated and oiled grill and grill it for about 5 to 10 min on each side.

9. Finally serve your grilled chicken legs with the rest of the marinade & enjoy.

Prep Time: 20 to 25 min

Cooking Time: 2 to 3 h

Servings: 4 to 6

If you're a legend, then make this one.

Nutritional information:

Calories: 749

Total Fat: 24.3 g

Protein: 121.3 g

Total Carbs: 5.5 g

Vintage Grilled Skirt Steak (Churrasco)

Being lucky is definitely better.

Ingredients:

- Chimichurri
- 1 teaspoon onion powder
- Sea salt and fresh ground black pepper
- Vegetable oil cooking spray
- About 1.5 tablespoon extra-virgin olive oil
- 1 tablespoon white wine vinegar
- 2 skirt steaks

Chimichurri Sauce:

- 4 cups flat-leaf parsley
- About 1/2 cup red wine vinegar
- Salt and freshly ground black pepper
- 1 heaping teaspoon red pepper flakes, optional
- 6 cloves garlic

- 3/4 cup extra-virgin olive oil

Directions:

1. First of all, please assemble all the ingredients at one place. Cut the steak into medium pieces.
2. Then to make the chimichurri sauce, combine the wine vinegar, red pepper flakes, black pepper, garlic, parsley & oil in a blender. Blend until smooth. Set aside for now.
3. This step is important. Add in the onion powder, wine vinegar, oil & black pepper in another bowl. Mix well.
4. Now rub the steak using the mixture & let it marinate for about 30 to 35 minutes or longer.
5. In the hot charcoal grill the steak for about 40 to 45 minutes.
6. One thing remains to be done. Then brush the onion mixture occasionally onto the steak.

7. Finally serve with the chimichurri sauce.

Mystery is unveiled!!

Lucky Raspberry BBQ Sauce

The speed matters…

Ingredients:

- 1/16 teaspoon onion powder
- 3 garlic cloves, peeled and crushed
- 1 1/4 cups raspberries
- 1/8 teaspoon salt
- About 3.5 tablespoons brown sugar, packed
- 1 tablespoon corn syrup, light
- 1 tablespoon balsamic vinegar
- 1/8 teaspoon ground black pepper
- About 1 teaspoon lemon juice
- 1 teaspoon molasses
- About 1/4 teaspoon red pepper flakes, properly crushed (add more or less depending on how spicy you want the sauce to be)
- 1/4 teaspoon olive oil

Directions:

1. First of all, please assemble all the ingredients at one place. Preheat the oven to about 410 to 420 degrees F. Line a baking sheet with thick aluminum foil.
2. Then lay the garlic on the baking sheet & drizzle oil on top.
3. Wrap the oil-covered garlic with the foil & bake in the oven for about 20 to 25 minutes.
4. Now please remove the baking sheet from the oven & then let it cool for about 10 to 15 minutes.
5. This step is important. Transfer the baked garlic to a saucepan along with the remaining ingredients.
6. Set the saucepan on the stove over medium heat.
7. Now bring the mixture to a boil before reducing heat & letting the sauce simmer for about 15 to 20 minutes or until it thickens.

8. Remove the sauce from the heat & let it cool down a bit. Next, please pour the sauce into a blender or even food processor.
9. Then pulse until the mixture is smooth, except for the seeds.
10. Using a strainer or a piece of cheesecloth, strain the seeds from the sauce.
11. One thing remains to be done. Use the sauce immediately or transfer to a mason jar.
12. Finally store unused sauce in the fridge for up to 10 days.

Serving: about 2 cups

Total Time: 50 to 60 minutes

Be super

Happy Beer Can Chicken with KC Rub

Deserved!!

Ingredients:

- 1/4 cup vegetable oil
- 1 cup cherry wood chips
- 1/2 cup paprika
- About 1 teaspoon cayenne pepper
- 1/4 cup kosher salt
- 1 half-filled can of beer
- 1/4 cup ground black peppercorns
- About 1 teaspoon cayenne powder
- 1 whole chicken

Directions:

1. First of all, please assemble all the ingredients at one place. Start by soaking the cherry wood chips in water for about an hour.

2. Now in a small bowl combine the paprika, peppercorns, salt, & cayenne powder.
3. Open beer & pour out approximately half of the contents.
4. Then add one teaspoon of the spice mixture into the can, adding it slowly to minimize foaming.
5. This step is important. Place the can in the middle of a small metal tray or baking sheet. Set aside.
6. Now please remove the giblets from inside the body cavity & then brush the vegetable oil over the entire chicken & then pat liberally with the remaining spice rub mixture.
7. Now after preparing the chicken, insert the beer can into the cavity with its legs at the bottom, & the chicken standing upright.
8. Place it, with the can, back onto the tray.
9. Prepare the grill and bring the heat to about 340 to 350°F.

10. Then drain the water from the cherry wood chips & add them to the grill.

11. Add the chicken onto the grill & cook properly for about 80 to 90 minutes, or until internal temperature measures 165°F in the breast or 180°F in the thigh area.

12. Now remove from heat & let rest for about 10 to 15 minutes.

13. One thing remains to be done. Make sure to wear protective covering on your hands when removing the can, as it will be very hot.

14. Finally use the contents of the can as a baste for the chicken, if desired.

Serves: 2 to 4

Long way to go…

Great Sliced Brisket Heroes with Memphis Slaw

Cooking level infinite....

Ingredients:

- 1/2 head cabbage, sliced (approximately 21/2 cups)
- 6 thin slices Muenster cheese
- 1/2 cup red onion (Diced)
- 1/2 cup carrot (Shredded)
- 1/2 cup pickle slices
- About 1/2 cup red bell pepper, finely diced
- About 1.5 tablespoon brown sugar
- 1/2 cup Classic Memphis BBQ sauce – optional (see recipe)
- 1 tablespoon paprika
- 1 medium tomato sliced
- 1 teaspoon celery seed
- About 1.5 teaspoon cumin
- 2 long hero sandwich rolls
- 1/4 cup apple cider vinegar

- 1/2 teaspoon dry mustard
- About 1.5 tablespoon fresh chives
- 1 lb leftover smoked and grilled brisket
- 1/2 cup mayonnaise

Directions:

1. First of all, please assemble all the ingredients at one place. Cut the leftover brisket into thin slices.
2. Then toss with Classic Memphis BBQ sauce, if desired.
3. In a large bowl, combine the carrot, cabbage, onion, and red bell pepper. Toss to mix well.
4. This step is important. In a small or medium bowl, combine the paprika, brown sugar, celery seed, dry mustard, cumin, & chives.
5. Now mix well, making sure brown sugar is not clumpy in the mixture.

6. Add in the mayonnaise & apple cider vinegar.
7. Whisk until well blended & smooth.
8. Then quickly add the dressing to the cabbage mixture & then toss to coat well.
9. Slice the sandwich rolls in half lengthwise.
10. Arrange the brisket on each of the rolls.
11. One thing remains to be done. Top with Muenster cheese, tomato, Memphis slaw, & pickle slices.
12. Finally place tops of rolls back on top & slice each in half.

Uber fantastic!!

Fantastic Beer Can Chicken

For those who are not ordinary, try this one.

Ingredients:

- About 2.5 tablespoons olive oil
- Salt and freshly ground pepper
- About 1 opened, half-full can of beer, room temperature.
- 1 lemon, halved & about 1 tablespoon of zest
- 2 tablespoons fresh thyme
- 1 sprig of rosemary
- About 1.5 tablespoon fresh oregano
- 1 whole chicken, about 4 pounds

Directions:

1. First of all, please assemble all the ingredients at one place. Set up the grill for indirect heat,

adjusting racks or placing coals to the sides.

2. Now clean chicken. Rub with the olive oil, oregano, thyme, lemon zest, salt & a generous grind of black pepper.

3. Put the rosemary sprig into the half can of beer.

4. This step is important. Squeeze the juice of the lemon into the can.

5. Then lower the chicken onto the can, leg-side down so that it stands upright on its own.

6. Now please place on the grill away from direct heat.

7. Now cover the grill & do not open for at least an hour.

8. One thing remains to be done. After one hour, check every 15 to 20 minutes until the meat thermometer reads 160 to 165ºF when inserted into thigh. (Juices will run clear when done.)

9. Finally carefully remove chicken from HOT can using a spatula and tongs. Let rest about 10 to 15 minutes.

Serves: 4 to 6

Be amazed ?

Delightful Red Army Sauce

Wow, just wow!!

Ingredients:

- 1 tablespoon Worcestershire sauce
- 2 tablespoons black pepper
- 1 cup molasses
- About 1.5 tablespoon thyme
- 2 tablespoons lemon juice
- 1 (5.5 ounce) can tomato juice
- 2 tablespoons liquid smoke flavoring
- 2 tablespoons onion powder
- 2 tablespoons garlic salt
- About 3.5 tablespoons Hungarian sweet paprika
- 1 tablespoon nutmeg
- 3 tablespoons Chinese five-spice powder
- 1 cup ketchup

Directions:

1. First of all, please assemble all the ingredients at one place. Now in a large saucepan, mix together your ingredients.
2. Then bring mixture to a boil, reduce heat to low & simmer for about 10 to 15 minutes.
3. Finally cool before serving.

Show time!!

Super Red Army Sauce

Feast for you!!

Ingredients:

- 1 tablespoon Worcestershire sauce
- 2 tablespoons black pepper
- 1 cup molasses
- 1 tablespoon thyme
- About 2.5 tablespoons lemon juice
- 1 (5.5 ounce) can tomato juice
- 2 tablespoons liquid smoke flavoring
- 2 tablespoons onion powder
- 2 tablespoons garlic salt
- 3 tablespoons Hungarian sweet paprika
- About 1.5 tablespoon nutmeg
- 3 tablespoons Chinese five-spice powder
- 1 cup ketchup

Directions:

1. First of all, please assemble all the ingredients at one place. Then in a large saucepan, mix together your ingredients.
2. Now bring mixture to a boil, reduce heat to low & simmer for about 10 to 15 minutes.
3. Finally cool before serving.

Being super is a matter of recipe... ?

Awesome Barbecued asparagus with prosciutto

Being a legend.

Ingredients:

- 5 to 6 slices Primo Gourmet Selection Prosciutto, which are thinly sliced lengthways
- About 2.5 bunches asparagus, woody ends trimmed

Directions:

1. First of all, please assemble all the ingredients at one place. Now quickly wrap a slice of prosciutto around an asparagus spear.
2. Now please repeat with remaining prosciutto & asparagus.
3. Preheat barbecue on high.
4. One thing remains to be done. Then cook asparagus on barbecue, turning occasionally, for about 5 to 10 minutes or until just tender.

5. Finally serve on a platter with baby potato rosemary skewers.

When you're fantastic, this is best!!

Iconic Summertime Dinner Hens

Being rich is a plus point ?

Ingredients:

- 4 fresh rosemary sprigs
- 4 teaspoons chicken rub
- About 4.5 tablespoons melted butter
- 4 Cornish game hens

Directions:

1. First of all, please assemble all the ingredients at one place. Preheat the pallet grill to about 360 to 370 degrees F.
2. Now with paper towels, pat dry hens.
3. Tuck the wings behind the backs & with kitchen strings, tie the legs together.
4. This step is important. Coat the outside of each hen with melted butter & sprinkle with rub evenly.

5. Then stuff the cavity of each hen with a rosemary sprig.
6. One thing remains to be done. Place the hens in pallet grill & cook properly for about 50 to 60 minutes.
7. Finally remove the hens from pallet grill & transfer onto a platter for about 5 to 10 minutes before serving.

Amazing cooking starts here...

Per Serving:

Calories: 311

Fat: 25.9g

Carbs: 1.1g

Protein: 17g

Ultimate Smoked Turkey Legs

Don't forget this one...

Ingredients:

- Salt
- 1 cup of distilled water
- Black pepper
- About 3.5 tablespoons of dark brown sugar
- 1 teaspoon of Prague powder 1
- About 1.5 tablespoon of kosher salt
- 2 large turkey drumsticks

Directions:

1.   First of all, please assemble all the ingredients at one place. Now

preheat the smoker on 310 to 320 F.

2. One thing remains to be done. Whisk the sugar with water, salt & Prague powder until they dissolve then Pour it in a large zip lock bag with the turkey legs & refrigerate it for 12 h.

3. Finally drain the turkey legs & smoke them for 1 h or until they register 160 F.

Prep Time: 10 to 15 min

Cooking Time: 1 h

Servings: 2 to 4

Sizzle your taste buds…

Nutritional information:

Calories: 630

Total Fat: 17 g

Protein: 99.6 g

Total Carbs: 13.2 g

Unique Churrasco Steak Kebab with Chimichurri sauce

Legends are born in…

Ingredients:

Steak Kebabs (churrasco):

- 500g of thick cut sirloin steak

Chimichurri Marinade:

- 100g parsley finely chopped
- 1 clove garlic crushed
- About 1.5 tablespoon red wine vinegar
- Juice of 1/2 lemon
- 1 tablespoon dried oregano
- Couple pinches of sea salt and pepper
- About 4.5 tablespoon extra virgin olive oil
- Pinch dried chili flakes
- 3 cherry tomatoes finely chopped

Directions:

1. First of all, please assemble all the ingredients at one place. To quickly make the marinade, please combine all the ingredients in a blender.
2. Then blend for about 30 to 35 seconds or until you get a smooth mixture.
3. This step is important. Cut the sirloin steak into smaller pieces.
4. Now coat the steak in the marinade & put it in the refrigerator for about 2.5 hours.
5. Use skewers to thread the meat.
6. One thing remains to be done. Grill them in the hot charcoal for about 5 to 10 minutes or so.
7. Finally serve hot.

Preparation Time: 2 hours

Cooking Time: 10 to 15 minutes

Servings: 2 to 4

Jaw dropping!!

Yummy Plum BBQ Sauce

Speed defines it…

Ingredients:

- 1/4 teaspoon red pepper flakes
- 1/3 cup brown sugar, packed
- About 1/2 teaspoon garlic powder
- 1/3 cup ketchup
- 1 teaspoon Worcestershire sauce
- 1/2 teaspoon salt
- About 2.5 tablespoons apple cider vinegar
- 1/2 teaspoon ground black pepper
- 1 cup chopped plums

Directions:

1. First of all, please assemble all the ingredients at one place. Then

quickly place all the ingredients in a food processor.

2. Then pulse until the mixture is smooth.

3. Transfer the mixture to a saucepan & set on the stove over medium heat.

4. This step is important. Now please let the mixture reduce by about 1/3 to 1/2 while stirring frequently.

5. Now this should take about 10 to 18 minutes.

6. One thing remains to be done. Now quickly remove the saucepan from the stove & then let it cool a bit before pouring the sauce into a mason jar.

7. Finally store in the fridge until ready to use.

Serving: about 1 1/2 cups

Total Time: 20 to 30 minutes

Mystery with this recipe or rather a chemistry with it.

Tasty Buttermilk-Fried Chicken Sliders

Awesomeness fully loaded…

Ingredients:

- 1/2 cup carrot, shredded
- 8-10 slider-sized sandwich buns or buttermilk biscuits
- 1 cup buttermilk
- About 1.5 teaspoon ground celery seed
- 1 clove garlic, crushed and minced
- 1 tablespoon sugar
- 1/2 cup mayonnaise
- About 1 cup prepared cayenne hot sauce
- 2 pounds boneless chicken breasts
- 1/4 cup vinegar

Directions:

1. First of all, please assemble all the ingredients at one place. Gently pound the chicken breasts so that they all have an even thickness.
2. Now cut the chicken breast into approximately 8 pieces, appropriately sized for slider sandwiches.
3. Now depending on the size & the thickness of your chicken breast you may end up with a slightly different number of servings.
4. Then in a medium-sized bowl, combine the buttermilk with the garlic, sugar, & hot sauce.
5. This step is important. Add the chicken pieces and marinate for at least 20 to 25 minutes.
6. In another bowl combine the shredded carrots with the

mayonnaise, vinegar, & ground celery seed.

7. Now toss to coat well.

8. Cover and refrigerate until ready to use.

9. Prepare the grill and bring the heat to about 240 to 250°F.

10.   Then add chicken patties to the grill and cook for approximately 20 to 25 minutes, flipping once halfway through.

11.   One thing remains to be done. Near the end of the cooking time please add the slider buns to the grill and toast for about 2 minutes, if desired.

12.   Finally remove from grill, place on buns & serve with chilled carrot slaw. Serve immediately.

Now the wait is over for hungry people.

Titanic Lazy Memphis Night Meatloaf

Magical, isn't it?

Ingredients:

- 1/2 cup Whistlin' Whiskey Grilling Sauce –optional (see recipe)
- 11/2 cups crushed crackers (saltine or butter crackers work fine)
- 1/2 cup yellow onion (Diced)
- About 1/2 teaspoon cayenne powder
- 2 tablespoons milk
- 1/4 cup celery diced
- 1/4 cup red bell pepper (Diced)
- 1 egg
- 1/2 lb ground pork
- 1 teaspoon thyme
- About 1.5 teaspoon paprika

- 1 teaspoon garlic powder
- 1 lb ground beef
- 1 teaspoon brown sugar

Directions:

1. First of all, please assemble all the ingredients at one place. Clean and prepare grill.
2. Now heat grill to approximately 290 to 300°F.
3. In a large bowl, combine the beef, onion, pork, crackers, celery, and red pepper. Mix thoroughly.
4. Then add in the egg, milk, brown sugar, paprika, garlic powder, thyme, and cayenne powder. Mix well.
5. This step is important. Place the meatloaf mixture onto a large piece of foil. Form a loaf in the center using your hands.

6. Brush with Whistlin' Whiskey Grilling Sauce, if desired.

7. Now roll the sides of the foil up around the meatloaf to form a sort of a pan.

8. Do not completely cover the top of the meatloaf.

9. Place the meatloaf in the foil onto the grill.

10. Then cook properly for about 1 to 11/2 hours, or until a meat thermometer inserted into the center reads 150 to 160°F.

11. One thing remains to be done. Remove from heat & let rest 10 to 15 minutes before serving.

12. Finally serve with extra sauce if desired.

Serves: 4 to 5

Yeah, it is a vintage recipe.

Rich BBQ Chicken Quarters

Always the upper hand…

Ingredients:

- 1 cup All-Purpose Chicken & Fish Marinade (recipe follows)
- Salt and freshly ground pepper
- About 1 cup onion (Chopped)
- 2 tablespoons Worcestershire sauce
- 1/2 cup ketchup
- 1/3 cup honey
- About 1.5 teaspoon chili powder
- 1/2 teaspoon ground mustard
- 4 chicken legs with thighs attached

Directions:

1. First of all, please assemble all the ingredients at one place.

Rinse chicken. Rub salt & pepper into the chicken quarters.

2. Then pour All-Purpose Chicken & Fish Marinade on quarters.

3. Marinate for about 3.5 hours in the refrigerator.

4. Take quarters out of the refrigerator about 20 to 25 minutes before cooking.

5. This step is important. Combine all remaining ingredients in a mixing bowl & stir until blended. Reserve.

6. Now light grill to medium-high or until coals have started to turn white.

7. Place on grill & cook properly for about 10 to 15 minutes.

8. Turn chicken over & baste with half of the BBQ sauce.

9. Then cook properly an additional 9–12 minutes.

10. Remove from grill & baste with remaining sauce.

11. One thing remains to be done. For indoor preparation, place chicken quarters in a deep baking pan and pour BBQ sauce over them, coating well.
12. Finally place in 400ºF oven & bake for about 50 to 55 minutes, basting occasionally.

Serves: 4 to 6

Now you're happy...?

Elegant Canadian Thin Maple BBQ Sauce

Classic style…

Ingredients:

- 1/2 cup cider vinegar
- 2 tablespoons aniseed
- 1/2 cup maple syrup
- About 1.5 teaspoon white pepper
- 1 tablespoon brown sugar
- 1/4 cup hot sauce
- 4 tablespoons all-purpose pork seasoning
- About 1.5 tablespoon sage
- 1 tablespoon red pepper flakes
- 1 cup white vinegar

Directions:

1. First of all, please assemble all the ingredients at one place. Now in a

large saucepan, mix together your ingredients.

2. Then bring mixture to a boil, reduce heat to low & simmer for about 10 to 15 minutes.

3. Finally cool before serving.

Arrive in style with this recipe.

Wonderful Canadian Thin Maple BBQ Sauce

Ironic in taste…

Ingredients:

- 1/2 cup cider vinegar
- 2 tablespoons aniseed
- 1/2 cup maple syrup
- About 1.5 teaspoon white pepper
- 1 tablespoon brown sugar
- 1/4 cup hot sauce
- 4 tablespoons all-purpose pork seasoning
- About 1.5 tablespoon sage
- 1 tablespoon red pepper flakes
- 1 cup white vinegar

Directions:

1. First of all, please assemble all the ingredients at one place. Then in a

large saucepan, mix together your ingredients.

2. Now bring mixture to a boil, reduce heat to low & simmer for about 5 to 10 minutes.

3. Finally cool before serving.

Looking forward to this one!!

Quick Teriyaki tofu kebabs

Used to eat this one a lot.

Ingredients:

- 2 zucchinis, cut into 2cm pieces
- 210ml teriyaki & roasted garlic marinade
- 320g firm tofu, cut into 16
- 8 button mushrooms, halved

Directions:

1. First of all, please assemble all the ingredients at one place. Now please soak bamboo skewers in water for about 20 to 30 minutes to avoid burning during cooking.
2. Then quickly thread mushrooms, zucchini & tofu alternately onto bamboo skewers.
3. Place prepared kebabs into glass dish.

4. This step is important. Pour teriyaki marinade over kebabs & refrigerate for about 20 to 25 minutes.
5. Now heat barbeque or grill plate over a medium heat.
6. Place kebabs onto hot plate or grill.
7. One thing remains to be done. Turn kebabs to ensure even cooking. Cook properly for about 5 to 10 minutes.
8. Finally drizzle kebabs with any remaining marinade & serve with fried rice.

There it is.

Awesome Favorite Whole Turkey

Tasty dish just one step away!!

Ingredients:

- 1/4 cup olive oil
- About 2.5 tablespoons honey
- Salt & freshly ground black pepper, to taste
- About 2.5 tablespoons apple cider vinegar
- 1 cup chicken broth
- 1 (15-pound) neck and giblets removed whole turkey

Directions:

1. First of all, please assemble all the ingredients at one place. Preheat the pallet grill to about 260 to 270 degrees F.
2. Now arrange a rack in a large roasting pan.

3. Place turkey over rack in roasting pan.
4. Coat the turkey with oil generously & then season with salt and black pepper evenly.
5. This step is important. Place the roasting pan in pallet grill & cook properly for about 40 to 45 minutes.
6. Then meanwhile in a bowl, mix together remaining ingredients.
7. After 40 to 45 minutes, coat the turkey with honey mixture.
8. Cook properly for about 3 to 4 hours, coating with honey mixture after every 40 to 45 minutes.
9. One thing remains to be done. Remove turkey from pallet grill & transfer onto a cutting board for about 15 to 20 minutes before carving.
10. Finally with a sharp knife, cut the turkey in desired sized pieces and serve.

I was waiting for this one.

Per Serving:

Calories: 761

Fat: 14.5g

Carbs: 2.3g

Protein: 124.9g

Legendary Smoked Turkey Breast

Silently waiting...

Ingredients:

- The zest of 1 lemon
- 12 cups of water
- 3/4 cup of kosher salt
- About 1.5 clove of garlic, crushed
- 1 shallot, finely chopped
- 4 bay leaves
- 10 thyme sprigs
- 8 sage leaves
- 6 pounds turkey breast

Directions:

1. First of all, please assemble all the ingredients at one place.

Rinse the turkey breast & set it aside.

2. Now please mix the rest of the ingredients in a medium or large bowl to make the brine.

3. This step is important. Now place the turkey breast in a large zip lock bag & pour the brine all over it then seal the bag and refrigerate it for about 7.5 h to an overnight.

4. Then preheat the smoker on 190 to 200 F.

5. One thing remains to be done. Place the turkey breast in the smoker & smoke it for about 3 to 4 h.

6. Finally once the time is up, remove the breast from the smoker & wrap it tightly in a piece of foil then allow it to rest for about 20 to 25 min then serve it & enjoy.

Prep Time: 20 to 25 min

Cooking Time: 3 to 4 h

Servings 10 to 12

I know, this is amazing!!

Nutritional information:

Calories: 236

Total Fat: 3.8 g

Protein: 38.7 g

Total Carbs: 9.6 g

Excellent Lechon Liempo or Filipino Roasted Pork Belly

Silently, you were waiting for this one. Don't lie… ?

Ingredients:

- 2 tablespoons minced garlic
- 2 teaspoons freshly ground black pepper
- About 1.5 tablespoon white vinegar
- 2 tablespoons salt
- About 4.5 tablespoons olive oil
- 1 (5-lb) piece pork belly

Directions:

1. First of all, please assemble all the ingredients at one place. Combine the garlic, vinegar, oil, pepper & salt in a small bowl.
2. Then mix well & set aside for now.

3. This step is important. Now please discard the skin of the pork belly & then cut it into small pieces.
4. Rub the garlic vinegar mixture onto the pork.
5. One thing remains to be done. Now add charcoal to a chimney & grill the pork for about 5 to 10 minutes.
6. Finally serve hot.

Preparation Time: 15 to 20 minutes

Cooking Time: 10 to 15 minutes

Servings: 10 to 12

Make it quickly.

Astonishing Apricot BBQ Sauce

Supreme level.

Ingredients:

- 1 tablespoon red wine vinegar
- 3 tomatoes (Diced)
- 1 yellow onion (Minced)
- About 1/2 teaspoon ground cloves
- 1 jalapeno pepper, seeded and diced
- 5 garlic cloves (Minced)
- 1 cup brown sugar, packed
- 1 tablespoon Worcestershire sauce
- 2 cups apple cider vinegar
- About 1.5 tablespoon soy sauce
- 1/4 cup white wine
- 2 tablespoons spicy brown mustard
- 2 pounds apricots, pitted and halved

Directions:

1. First of all, please assemble all the ingredients at one place. Roast the onion, garlic, tomatoes, and jalapeno peppers in an oven at about 340 to 350 degrees F or so for about 25 to 30 minutes or until soft.
2. Then quickly transfer the roasted vegetables to a large pot.
3. Stir in the apricots, followed by the remaining ingredients.
4. Place the pot on the stove over medium-high heat.
5. This step is important. Allow the mixture to boil while stirring frequently.
6. Now reduce the heat & let the mixture simmer for 2 hours, making sure to stir every so often.
7. One thing remains to be done. You want the sauce to have a consistency similar to traditional BBQ sauce.

8. Finally remove the sauce from the heat & let it cool down a bit before transferring to mason jars.

Serving: 4 to 5 half-pint jars

Total Time: 2 hours 40 minutes

Sincere efforts will be awesome.

Great Lemon Pepper BBQ Grilled Chicken

Let's dive in…

Ingredients:

- Lemon wedges to garnish
- 2 cloves garlic, thinly sliced
- 1 lemon, sliced into wedges
- About 1.5 tablespoon Worcestershire sauce
- 1 teaspoon ground black peppercorns
- 1 cup tomato ketchup
- 1 cup tomato ketchup
- 1/2 cup apple cider vinegar
- About 1/2 cup brown sugar
- 4 boneless chicken breasts

Directions:

1. First of all, please assemble all the ingredients at one place. Place the chicken in a large bowl.
2. Now please squeeze the lemon juice over the chicken & sprinkle with black peppercorns.
3. Next, please add garlic and toss in the bowl, making sure that each piece of chicken is evenly coated.
4. Then cover & refrigerate for at least 2 hours.
5. This step is important. While the chicken is marinating, prepare the barbecue sauce. In a small or medium bowl, please combine the apple cider vinegar, brown sugar, ketchup & Worcestershire sauce.
6. Mix well & then set aside or refrigerate until ready to use.
7. Now quickly prepare the grill and bring the heat to about 290 to 300°F.

8. Next, please remove the chicken from the marinade & then place on the grill.
9. Next, cook the chicken for about 15 to 18 minutes & then baste with the prepared sauce, coating the top side, then flipping & coating the other.
10.   Then continue to grill for another 10 to 15 minutes or until the juices run clear & the internal temperature reaches 165-170°F.
11.   One thing remains to be done. Now please remove from heat & let rest 5 to 10 minutes before serving.
12.   Finally garnish with lemons & squeeze additional fresh lemon juice over the chicken, if desired.

Serves: 3 to 4

Your friends and family are waiting. Hurry!!

Happy Smokey BBQ Chicken and Bottom Barrel Baked Beans

Royal taste…

Ingredients:

- 1 teaspoon dry mustard
- About 2.5 tablespoons olive oil
- Taste of Memphis Rub (see recipe here)
- 2 tablespoons paprika
- 1 tablespoon butter
- 1/2 cup red onion (Diced)
- 4 cloves garlic, minced and crushed
- 1/4 cup dark beer
- 1 small jalapeño pepper, diced finely
- 2 28-ounce cans prepared baked beans
- 1/4 cup apple cider vinegar
- About 1 cup brown sugar
- 1/2 cup ketchup
- 4 lbs skin-on chicken pieces
- 3 tablespoons molasses

Directions:

1. First of all, please assemble all the ingredients at one place. Begin by cleaning and preparing grill.
2. Now heat to approximately 260 to 275°F.
3. Brush the chicken with the olive oil & apply the Taste of Memphis Rub.
4. Then place chicken on the grill & cook properly for approximately 11/2 hours, turning every 30 to 35 minutes and applying more rub, if desired.
5. This step is important. Preheat oven to 290 to 300°F.
6. In a Dutch oven, please melt butter over medium heat.
7. Now add the garlic, red onion, and jalapeño pepper.
8. Sauté until tender & fragrant, approximately 2 to 5 minutes.
9. Add the beans and the remaining ingredients. Mix well.

10. Continue stirring while cooking over medium heat for about 5 to 10 minutes or until brown sugar is completely dissolved.
11. Then cover and place the beans in the oven.
12. One thing remains to be done. Bake for about 25 to 30 minutes.
13. Finally remove from oven & let sit 5 to 10 minutes before serving with grilled chicken.

Serves: 4 to 6

We all are legends in some ways.

Lucky All-Purpose Chicken & Fish Marinade

Prepare yourself for this...

Ingredients:

- 1 cup high-quality extra virgin olive oil
- 2 tablespoons fresh parsley, chopped
- 4 cloves garlic, finely minced
- About 1.5 tablespoon fresh thyme (Chopped)
- 3 shallots, finely minced
- 2 green onions, finely minced
- About 1.5 tablespoon brown sugar
- 3 lemons, juiced and zested
- 3 limes, juiced and zested
- 1 lidded 16-ounce jar
- 6 tablespoons Dijon mustard

Directions:

1. First of all, please assemble all the ingredients at one place. Now combine all ingredients into lidded jar.
2. Finally shake well until mixture thickens & is well blended.

Serves: about 2 cups

Looking forward to healthy life.

Vintage Alcatraz BBQ Sauce

Astonishing!!

Ingredients:

- 2 tablespoons sea salt/kosher salt
- 1/2 cup brown sugar
- 3/4 cup cider vinegar
- About 2.5 tablespoons black pepper
- 3/4 cup beer
- 1 tablespoon cinnamon
- 4 tablespoons serrano chile powder
- 2 tablespoons taco seasoning mix
- 3 tablespoons turmeric
- About 3.5 tablespoons lemon pepper
- 2 tablespoons rosemary
- 11/2 cups prepared yellow mustard

Directions:

1. First of all, please assemble all the ingredients at one place. Now in a large saucepan, mix together your ingredients.
2. Then bring mixture to a boil, reduce heat to low & simmer for about 10 to 15 minutes.
3. Finally cool before serving.

Grab it!!

Best Alcatraz BBQ Sauce

Freshness loaded!!

Ingredients:

- 1/2 cup brown sugar
- 2 tablespoons sea salt/kosher salt
- 3/4 cup cider vinegar
- 2 tablespoons black pepper
- 3/4 cup beer
- About 1.5 tablespoon cinnamon
- 2 tablespoons taco seasoning mix
- 4 tablespoons serrano chile powder
- 3 tablespoons turmeric
- About 3.5 tablespoons lemon pepper
- 2 tablespoons rosemary
- 11/2 cups prepared yellow mustard

Directions:

1. First of all, please assemble all the ingredients at one place. Now in a large saucepan, mix together your ingredients.
2. Then bring mixture to a boil, reduce heat to low & simmer for about 10 to 15 minutes.
3. Finally cool before serving.

Dreams are good!! So dream about this one or else make it...

Nostalgic Pepper steak with tomatoes

Something is definitely different.

Ingredients:

- 4 (250g each) beef sirloin steaks, trimmed
- potato salad, to serve
- About 2.5 tablespoons cracked black pepper
- 1 bunch rocket, trimmed
- olive oil cooking spray
- 500g truss cherry tomatoes
- About 1.5 tablespoon olive oil

Directions:

1. First of all, please assemble all the ingredients at one place. Rub both sides' steaks with oil.
2. Then place pepper on a plate.
3. Press steaks into pepper to lightly coat.

4. Preheat a barbecue grill on medium-high heat.
5. This step is important. Barbecue steaks for about 2 to 5 minutes each side for medium or until cooked to your liking. Transfer to a plate.
6. Now cover with foil and set aside for about 5 to 10 minutes to rest.
7. Meanwhile, spray tomatoes with oil.
8. Barbecue tomatoes, turning occasionally, for about 2 to 5 minutes or until just tender.
9. One thing remains to be done. Then arrange rocket on serving plates.
10. Finally serve steaks with tomatoes & potato salad.

This is epic. Take a look!!

Mighty Thanksgiving Turkey

Life of a legend begins here.

Ingredients:

- 1 quartered onion
- About 2.5 tablespoons seasoned salt
- 1/2 cup softened butter
- Salt & freshly ground black pepper, to taste
- 1 (10-pound) neck and giblets removed whole turkey
- 4 crushed garlic cloves
- 1 cored and quartered apple

Directions:

1. First of all, please assemble all the ingredients at one place. Preheat the pallet grill to 225 to 250 degrees F.
2. Now for stuffing in a bowl, mix together apple, butter, onion, salt and black pepper.

3. Rub the crushed garlic over the outer side of turkey evenly & then, sprinkle with seasoned salt.
4. This step is important. Stuff the cavity of turkey with apple mixture.
5. Then arrange the turkey in a disposable roasting pan & with a piece of foil, cover the roasting pan loosely.
6. Place the roasting pan in pallet grill & cook properly for about 10 to 15 minutes, basting with pan juices after every 1 hour.
7. One thing remains to be done. Now remove turkey from pallet grill & transfer onto a cutting board for about 15 to 20 minutes before carving.
8. Finally with a sharp knife, cut the turkey in desired sized pieces & serve.

Funny but definitely yummy!!

Per Serving:

Calories: 729

Fat: 25.6g

Carbs: 8.1g

Protein: 52g

King sized Beer Chicken

Now that's something!!

Ingredients:

- 12 ounces of beer
- Salt
- About 2.5 tablespoon of brown sugar
- Black pepper
- 2 tablespoons of chili powder
- About 1.5 tablespoon of olive oil
- 2 (4 pounds each) whole chicken

Directions:

1. First of all, please assemble all the ingredients at one place. Preheat the smoker on 190 to 200 F.

2. Now rinse the chicken & pat it dry then season it with some salt and pepper.

3. This step is important. Now please mix the rest of the ingredients in a small or medium bowl & then rub the chicken with it.

4. One thing remains to be done. Then refrigerate the chicken & allow it to marinate for 20 min then place it in the smoker and smoke it for about 3 to 4 h or until it registers 165 F.

5. Finally once the time is up, grill the chicken for about 5 to 10 min on each side then serve them & warm and enjoy.

Prep Time: 10 to 15 min

Cooking Time: 3 to 4 h

Servings 5 to 8

Can you make it? Yes, why not?

Nutritional information:

Calories: 733

Total Fat: 15.8 g

Protein: 131.9 g

Total Carbs: 4.8 g

Crazy Filipino Skewered Banana ketchup Pork Shoulder BBQ

Good days!!

Ingredients:

- 1/4 teaspoon salt
- About 1.5 tablespoon garlic powder
- 3/4 cup soy sauce
- 3/4 cup banana ketchup
- 1/2 cup brown sugar
- About 1 teaspoon ground black pepper
- Juice from 2 lemons
- 4 lbs pork shoulder

Directions:

1. First of all, please assemble all the ingredients at one place. Cut the pork shoulder into small pieces.
2. Now in a bowl combine the brown sugar with lemon juice. Stir until sugar dissolves.

3. This step is important. Add in the banana ketchup, soy sauce, salt, pepper, and garlic powder.
4. Then mix well & marinate the pork shoulder for 1 hour.
5. Use soaked bamboo skewers to thread the pork pieces.
6. One thing remains to be done. Grill the pork skewers under hot charcoal for about 5 to 10 minutes on each side.
7. Finally serve hot.

Preparation Time: 1.5 hours

Cooking Time: 10 to 15 minutes

Servings: 8 to 12

I am interested!!

Pinnacle Mango-Habanero BBQ Sauce

This never goes out of style.

Ingredients:

- 1/4 teaspoon salt
- 2 habanero chilies, destemmed
- 1/2 cup carrot, sliced thinly
- About 2.5 tablespoons lime juice
- 1/2 small yellow onion
- About 2.5 tablespoons apple cider vinegar
- 1 garlic cloves (Minced)
- 3/4 cup mango (Diced)

Directions:

1. First of all, please assemble all the ingredients at one place. Prepare the habanero by removing the seeds – the more seeds, the hotter it is.

2. Now place all the ingredients, including the pepper from Step 1, into a food processor & pulse until the mixture is smooth.
3. This step is important. Pour the smooth mixture into a saucepan & set on the stove over medium-high heat.
4. Then once the mixture starts to boil, reduce the heat & let it simmer.
5. Now let the mixture simmer for about 10 to 15 minutes.
6. Now remove the saucepan from the heat & let the sauce cool down a bit.
7. One thing remains to be done. Pour the sauce into a mason jar.
8. Finally store any unused sauce in the fridge for 7 to 10 days.

Serving: 10 to 12

Total Time: 30 to 40 minutes

Now be a legend!!

Perfect Barbecued Wild Turkey

Simple yet fantastic!!

Ingredients:

- 1/2 cup soy sauce
- About 1/2 teaspoon hot sauce
- 1/2 cup water
- 1 tablespoon lemon juice
- 2 tablespoons brown sugar
- 1/4 cup peppercorns
- About 2.5 tablespoons olive oil
- 1 wild turkey breast

Directions:

1. First of all, please assemble all the ingredients at one place. Begin by slicing the turkey breasts into strips that are approximately 1/2 inch thick.

2. Now in a bowl, combine the remaining ingredients to make a marinade & mix well.

3. Place sliced turkey breast in a pan & pour the marinade over the meat.

4. Then toss to make sure the marinade is evenly distributed.

5. This step is important. Now please cover & refrigerate at least 4 hours, or overnight if possible.

6. Prepare the grill and bring the heat to about 250 to 270°F.

7. Now drain the meat, reserving about 1/4 cup of the marinade to use as a baste.

8. Take care to avoid contamination by making sure the brush you use to baste the turkey does not come in any contact with other foods, & also do not use this as a baste at the end of cooking.

9. Then only use about halfway through to add a bit more flavor.

10. One thing remains to be done. Place the sliced meat on the grill & cook properly for about 20 to 25 minutes, or until juices run clear, flipping once and basting halfway through.

11. Finally remove from heat & let rest 5 to 10 minutes before serving.

It is a brand new day…. Ever listened to this one!!

Dashing Dry Rubbed Chicken w/ Cornbread and Sausage Stuffing

Awesome, isn't it?

Ingredients:

- 2 lbs, bone-in chicken pieces with skin still attached
- 1 teaspoon white pepper
- About 2.5 tablespoons olive oil
- 1 teaspoon salt
- 2 tablespoons sweet paprika
- 2 tablespoons smoky paprika
- About 2.5 teaspoons oregano
- 3 teaspoons garlic powder
- 2 teaspoons celery salt
- 2 teaspoons chili powder
- Chicken

Stuffing

- 1 12oz box cornbread mix
- 1 egg, beaten
- About 2.5 tablespoons butter

- 1/2 cup onion, diced finely
- 1 cup chicken broth
- 1/2 cup celery diced finely
- 1/2 cup pecans, chopped
- 2 teaspoons sage
- 1 teaspoon pepper
- About 1.5 teaspoon thyme
- 1/2 lb pork sausage
- 1 teaspoon salt

Directions:

1. First of all, please assemble all the ingredients at one place. Begin by cleaning and preparing grill. Bring the heat to approximately 290 to 300°F.
2. Then in a small bowl, combine the ingredients for the dry rub: sweet paprika, celery salt, smoky paprika, garlic powder, chili powder, oregano, salt, & white pepper.
3. Mix thoroughly.

4. Now brush the chicken with the olive oil & pat the dry rub onto the chicken. Set aside.

5. This step is important. In a cast iron skillet, please brown the sausage.

6. Drain and set aside.

7. In the same skillet, melt the butter over medium heat.

8. Then add the celery, onion, and pecans.

9. Now please cook until onion begins to soften, approximately 3 to 5 minutes.

10. Now quickly add the sausage back into the pan & season with sage, thyme, salt and pepper.

11. Now reduce heat to low.

12. Meanwhile, in a bowl, combine the cornbread mix, chicken broth, & egg. Mix thoroughly.

13. Pour mixture into skillet & mix with sausage mixture.

14. Then remove from heat & cover with foil.

15. Place both the chicken & the skillet onto the hot grill.

16. One thing remains to be done. Cook properly both for approximately 1.5 hours or until a meat thermometer inserted into the chicken reads 160°F, & the stuffing is cooked through.

17. Finally remove from heat & let rest 5 to 10 minutes before serving.

Serves: 4 to 6

Luxury tasty dish for you!!

Reliable Whole Spit-Grilled Chicken

Get ready to make it my way!!

Ingredients:

- 1 carrot, cut in half
- Olive oil
- 1 celery stalk, cut in half
- About 1 teaspoon black pepper
- 1/4 of an onion
- 1 lemon (Sliced)
- 1/2 teaspoon salt
- 4 cloves garlic
- 1 teaspoon fresh thyme
- 1 tablespoon dried parsley
- About 1.5 teaspoon paprika
- 1/2 teaspoon cumin
- 1/4 teaspoon turmeric
- 1 chicken, about 4 pounds

Directions:

1. First of all, please assemble all the ingredients at one place. Rinse, clean & dry the chicken.
2. Now place the onion, carrot, celery, lemon slices and garlic in the cavity.
3. Truss the chicken, insert spit & secure.
4. This step is important. Stir together thyme, parsley, paprika, cumin, turmeric, salt and pepper.
5. Then rub chicken with olive oil; sprinkle with herb mixture & rub into skin.
6. Grill chicken on rotisserie about 1 1/2 hours at around 300ºF.
7. One thing remains to be done. Brush with wet mop (recipe follows) every 30 to 35 minutes.
8. Finally internal temperature of thickest part of the thigh should be 165ºF.

Serves: 4 to 6

The best combo ever!!

Charming Smokey Coffee Sauce

Something is new here!!

Ingredients:

- 1 medium onion, chopped
- 2 tablespoons black pepper
- 1/4 cup white vinegar
- 1/2 cup water
- About 2.5 tablespoons caraway seeds
- 1/4 cup vegetable oil
- 1/2 cup ketchup
- 2 tablespoons mustard seed (Ground)
- 2 tablespoons Worcestershire sauce
- 11/2 teaspoons liquid smoke flavoring
- 2 tablespoons brown sugar
- 2 tablespoons nutmeg
- About 1.5 tablespoon prepared mustard

- 1 tablespoon dry mesquite seasoning mix
- 4 tablespoons coffee beans (Ground)
- 2 tablespoons lemon juice

Directions:

1. First of all, please assemble all the ingredients at one place. Then in a large saucepan, mix together your ingredients.
2. Now bring mixture to a boil, reduce heat to low & simmer for about 10 to 15 minutes.
3. Finally cool before serving.

A little work here but will be worth it.

Energetic Smokey Coffee Sauce

Try it...

Ingredients:

- 1 medium onion, chopped
- 2 tablespoons black pepper
- 1/4 cup white vinegar
- About 2.5 tablespoons caraway seeds
- 1/2 cup water
- 1/4 cup vegetable oil
- 1/2 cup ketchup
- 2 tablespoons mustard seed (Ground)
- 2 tablespoons Worcestershire sauce
- 11/2 teaspoons liquid smoke flavoring
- 2 tablespoons brown sugar
- About 2.5 tablespoons nutmeg
- 1 tablespoon prepared mustard
- 1 tablespoon dry mesquite seasoning mix

- 4 tablespoons coffee beans (Ground)
- 2 tablespoons lemon juice

Directions:

1. First of all, please assemble all the ingredients at one place. Now in a large saucepan, mix together your ingredients.
2. Then bring mixture to a boil, reduce heat to low & simmer for about 10 to 15 minutes.
3. Finally cool before serving.

This is different, isn't it?

Thanks for reading my book.

Made in the USA
Las Vegas, NV
28 February 2022